Compell
Providing Tools for Life

PASSION.
PURPOSE.
Time Management.

Finding your calling. Fine Tuning your life.

EmmaSara McMillion
Compelled Lifestyle Expert

Passion. Purpose. Time Management
Copyright 2017 Emma Sara McMillion

All rights reserved. No part of this publication may be reproduced, distributed, or transmitted in any form or by any means, including photocopying, recording, or other electronic or mechanical methods, without the prior written permission of the publisher, except in the case of brief quotations embodied in critical reviews and certain other noncommercial uses permitted by copyright law. For permission requests, write to the publisher, addressed "Attention: Permissions Coordinator," at the address below.

Unless otherwise indicated, all Scripture is taken from the English Standard Version (ESV). The Holy Bible, English Standard Version. ESV® Permanent Text Edition® (2016). Copyright © 2001 by Crossway Bibles, a publishing ministry of Good News Publishers.

New King James Version (NKJV). Scripture taken from the New King James Version®. Copyright © 1982 by Thomas Nelson. Used by permission. All rights reserved.King James Version (KJV). Public Domain. The Message (MSG) - Copyright © 1993, 1994, 1995, 1996, 2000, 2001, 2002 by Eugene H. Peterson

ISBN -13: 978-1545305072

Cover Designer: Jodi WilsonEditors: Lisa Thompson, Bijou McMillion
Vector Images Sourced: https://thenounproject.com
https://creativecommons.org/licenses/by/3.0/us/legalcode
Formatting by Rik – Wild Seas Formatting (WildSeasFormatting.com)

Compelled Lifestyle Publishing
PO BOX 1043
Alpine, TX 79831

The Noun Project Featured Artists:

Thinking by Artem, full circle by Trevor Mowry, checklist notepad by Karthik Srinivas, Strong Chain by Артур Абт, growth by Rockicon, Thinking by Alberto Guerra Quintanilla, crossed swords Yaroslav Samoilov, hear by Iván Andrés, fast by Marie Van den Broeck, clock Khomsun Chaiwong, flame Nadav Barkan.

"If you always do the same thing, you will always get the same result! Isn't it time to try something new?"

-EmmaSara

WELCOME TO A SHIFT IN THINKING!

The time for change is now!

_____

MY GUIDE MANUAL

_____

Date I started something **NEW**!

_____
_____

THIS INSIGHT IMPACTED ME THE MOST.

Dedication

This book is dedicated to my future generations, not yet born. May this book provide a blueprint for success in your lives and the lives of your children.

I also would like to dedicate this book to Yeshua, the Master Gardener, who has patiently cultivated this message within my heart. May He fertilize the words in these pages so that they bear much fruit.

I not only dedicate this book to my family, but I credit them with providing a rich learning environment for me to practice what I teach on a daily basis. To my husband, thank you for desiring to grow just as much I do and for all of your technical help on the book. To my children, thank you for the endless amount of help you gave around the house while I completed this manuscript and for your continued inspiration in my life. To my parents, thank you for sowing the seeds of integrity, hard work and perseverance into me at such an early stage in life.

To my friends, thank you for your support and constant feedback during the creative process.

Thank you, Jodi, for creating a perfect cover and for being so focused as we worked together.

Thank you, Lisa and Bijou for your hard work editing this book and for helping me "polish the gem."

Introduction
A Cultural Dilemma

Many business and motivational circles use the popular term, "know your why." What if I told you that "knowing your why" is only part of the equation for true success and not the full solution? I believe that people can have a strong "why" or reason for pursuing something yet still miss their unique calling. What if you only have part of the answer? What if you are missing the foundational portion?

Could it be possible that you may be off track and not even know it?

If you are like most people, you have a hunger and a desire to fulfill your highest calling in life, if you could only figure out what that calling is. When you stand back and look at the big picture, society appears to lack understanding about what defines one's true calling in life. Most people do not experience contentment, peace, or true joy in their lives. Some might experience momentary happiness, which is driven by circumstances. The joy that I speak of comes despite your circumstances. The greatest common denominator in our current culture is underlying confusion, which produces dis-ease and unrest in daily life. I live in a small town with some very old "Wild West" roots and hints of an era gone by when a man felt confident about what he was called to do. If you have ever met a real cowboy, a cowboy is as a cowboy does. They find great satisfaction in their lifestyle and occupation.

You can sense their passion. However, people often confuse their passion with their life's calling. I can relate as I certainly struggled with this for most of my life as well. As an extremely passionate individual and someone who is not easily influenced by others, I see succumbing to peer pressure as a sign of weakness. I don't have to go along with the crowd; as a matter of fact, I like to stand when no one else will stand. However, for the majority of my life, I confused my passions with my direct calling. Are you one of those people who think that passion equals calling? In the following chapters, I will explain the difference between the two and help you determine both your passion and your calling.

Table of Contents

Table of Contents 1
Chapter 1 3
   When You Are Driven by Passion ....
Chapter 2 17
   Identifying Calling ("What") vs. Passion ("Why") ....
Chapter 3 21
   Why Knowing Your "Why" Is NOT Enough! ....
Chapter 4 33
   Uniquely You ....
Chapter 5 41
   4 Steps to Find Your Calling—Your "What" ....
Chapter 6 71
   Making Time Deliver ....
Chapter 7 73
   Protecting Your Time ....
Chapter 8 81
   Step 2 Creating Goals ....
Chapter 9 95
   Step 3: Creating Safeguards ....
Chapter 10 103
   The Power of Multiplication ....
Chapter 11 113
   When Passion, Calling and Time Management Link up ....
Scriptures 123
   Identity in Christ ....
About the Author 127

Chapter 1

When You Are Driven by Passion

For years, I was driven by passion, and I thought I understood my purpose. However, through trials and life changing events I realized that my definition of a person's calling might be skewed.

My eyes were further opened when I stumbled onto a message that contained another piece to the **purpose puzzle.** The insight came one afternoon as I searched online for videos on time management. I listened to message after message on the subject. As I listened, I felt as if I were drinking from an old familiar cup that I had pulled out of the back of my cupboard. Obviously, the cup was available for use at any time, but it was pushed so far back into the cabinet that I forgot about it. As I listened to each lecture, I was not hearing too many new concepts. This left me thinking to myself, "*You know this stuff; why have you been dropping the ball for so long?*" It left me contemplating about the fact that I used much of this content for years and found it to be highly effective. Now, here I was, scratching my head about how I got to this point of "spinning plates" and running on a "hamster wheel" of life. I listened to one, then another, and another speaker, still with no big "aha" moments.

Finally, I listened to a young woman who captivated me with

her message. I found myself stopping and gravitating toward my computer screen so that I could completely soak in all that she was saying. My interest was piqued, and her calm and sincere presence grabbed my attention. I realized she was different because I could sense a true inner strength in her. She was just sharing her life and she had a loud message but it wasn't because she spoke with a loud voice. Instead, it was obvious to me that she had developed a firm standing. This sure footing allowed her to accomplish things that only a select group could do. She shared her story, her testimony, from her heart. It wasn't just another anecdote for time management that I already knew. What she had pierced my soul—an answer to something far greater than time management. After so many years she had the answer to my inner question, "What has caused me to hit the proverbial wall to further success?" I am typically good at evaluating situations and at self-examination, but apparently, I was missing something in the process. I was lacking awareness of my own motives. Now, here I was, listening and understanding something new about myself. It was as if I opened a foggy window, and now, I could clearly see! I listened as she shared her story of deep ocean diving. She was legit. She didn't wear an oxygen mask or any of the typical diving gear. No, instead, she held her breath for over 100 feet while spearfishing in a swimsuit! This woman possessed grit, yet she was confident and so inviting. She was someone with integrity and fortitude that you could sense deeply. I listened as she retold her childhood story. I could just image her snorkeling while her dad went spearfishing in the spectacular tropical ocean. It was apparent, watching her dad in that adventurous environment birthed her passion. Kimi Werner is no longer a little girl instead, she is a woman who has earned a powerful reputation in the world of spearfishing and has gone on to win many worldwide competitions. She really captured the spotlight when she went for the ride of her life holding on to the fin of a huge great white shark in the open ocean! After winning numerous awards and titles, **she also gained a strong vocal platform.** By shining in one area of her life, the media started to showcase her other passions and interests, including her cooking and her love for art. She was now given a voice to address various topics because **she gave her all to one area.** This struck a chord so deep within my soul that it moved me. Finally, I found a message that spoke straight to me, something I could identify with after all these months. I am a woman of so many passions and pursuits, yet I feel I have lacked focus in just one area. For many years, I have been operating a family blog that seems to be just hanging around. I admit that I have not given it the proper attention. The pattern is that I have so many interests that I tend to spread myself way too thin. I didn't want to just speak to one area but to many. The problem with that game plan is that I did not completely develop each area. I shied away from showcasing personal projects, probably because I ran after fame and accolades for so long that I saw it as a step back if I did anything to spotlight just me or my work. Every time I ventured out to do something with a self focus, I would take a step back and put the spotlight back on my family. I had been considering this issue for months. Now here I was, watching this woman share her testimony about harnessing time. Then, I had a **light bulb moment!** One reason I did not want to focus on one area is because I felt that by doing so, all the fire that is within me for other passions would somehow die down or fizzle away. When this epic spearfisher spoke the following words, it was as if she handed me an envelope with the solution inside. She said, "As soon as I focused on one thing and gave it my all, it opened up the door for everyone else to notice my other interests and passions." This statement struck a deep chord within me because she uncovered my unknown fear. The answer was now in front of me. I no longer suffered from a blind spot. **When you focus solely on one topic, you can gain a platform with a louder voice in other areas of importance.** I no longer had to worry that those areas might die or grow silent. To me, this spelled hope. I felt a release to focus on doing one thing well even if it meant leaving other subjects on the back burner for a while. **Release**—how sweet it is!

NOTES:

When you **FOCUS** solely on **ONE TOPIC,** you can **GAIN A PLATFORM** with a **LOUDER VOICE** in other areas of importance.

Kimi eventually quit entering contests when she realized that her passion and zeal no longer propelled her. She had been drawn to winning for winning's sake. She took a step back, surveyed her life, and found it wanting. Here she was, a worldwide winner in spearfishing, living a life that she thought she wanted, yet she was left feeling empty and unfulfilled. How could this be? This passion was developed during the sweetest times of her childhood. She was walking in the footsteps of her beloved father and traveling the globe as a winner with awards she earned by her fearlessness and drive. But now she had laid it all down. However, **by laying it down, she could now listen to her heart**. She could see that she got off track by pursuing rewards and trophies, rather than focusing on what birthed her childhood passion.

Winning athletes, such as boxers, train more than half their lives in an effort to find victory. Day and night, night and day, they train. They put their body under subjection to their mind to go the extra mile. They are willing to make sacrifices that the weekend athlete just won't make. **Winners have something in common—drive and tenacity. They pursue their prize and will not stop until they achieve victory!**

They train hard for that sweet taste of victory. The best of the best will not be moved by circumstances. When a world champion boxer is knocked down, he will get right back up and keep on fighting! His wounds cannot hold him down. The moment when he is lying on the mat, the world stops only momentarily. He doesn't call it quits. A champ has his eye on the prize, and even though he is shaken, his resolve surpasses the pain. He rises to fight again until he is victorious!

WINNERS have **DRIVE** and **TENACITY.** They **PURSUE** their prize & will **NOT STOP** until they achieve **VICTORY**.

Recently, I watched a replay clip of a historical fight between Mike Tyson and Buster Douglas. Mike was the undefeated, undisputed heavyweight champ of the world. Buster was in a bad spot, knocked down in the eighth round by Mike. He was officially in Mike's "no man's land," where Mike left 19 past opponents knocked out and down for the count. Now, here was Buster, his contender, a man who had just lost his mother 23 days earlier. As if that weren't bad enough, he entered the ring with the flu. The odds were stacked against him but, something awe-inspiring happened. He didn't give up! Buster arose! The world waited with bated breath as he got up to fight another two rounds and knocked out the world champion! Mike was bumped from his position, and a new victor was born.[1]

As I finished watching the clip, I focused on the power both of these men had. They arrived at a place in life where they taught their will and body to come into subjection to their mind. Buster's mind was on the prize. In the same way, the spearfisher had her mind on her prize with no lack of passion or zeal.

Where does the question of calling come into all of this? **No one can deny that all of these individuals possessed explosive passion, but were they following their calling?** I often tell my kids to ask themselves if something is a **good idea or a God idea.** Plenty of good ideas might be filled with passion galore, bu**t God does not always call us to a future position based on our previous passion.**

---

[1] https://en.wikipedia.org/wiki/Buster_Douglas. Accessed March 22, 2017.

PASSION. PURPOSE. TIME MANAGEMENT.

Often, He will call you out of your comfort zone to pursue a new thing.

Genesis 12:1 tells us how God did exactly that with Abra(ha)m and his family. "God told Abram: "Leave your country, your family, and your father's home for a land that I will show you." (The Message)

NOTES:

Are you willing **to step** out of your comfort zone to accomplish **GREAT THINGS?**

Abraham had no idea where he was going. All he knew was that Yahweh had called him to leave his father's land and he obeyed. God did not give him the specific details regarding the **new** land until he had left the **old** land—what was comfortable—behind.
Oh how I can relate!

Some people are pushed out of their comfort zone and are headed in the right direction while others can be pursuing something that is comfortable and be totally off track.

Each of the individuals just mentioned were clearly following their passion. Yet, did following their passions really serve them? Yes, they won titles, but did they win inner peace or contentment? Mike's former wife eventually charged him with spousal abuse and later in the ring he bit off a part of an opponent's ear. He had a winner's belt in the ring while struggling in life's arena. Buster Douglas accomplished a heroic feat that monumental day in the ring and kept his word to his mother that he would defeat Mike. However, he later suffered some real bumps in life, including serious addictions. He went on to overcome these obstacles and is now leading a productive life. Kimi became very discontented after all her wins when she temporarily lost her passion. However, she went on to find her true calling, her "what." So many people have it backwards. They are following their passions that are not rooted in their purpose. **Allow your purpose to become your passion. It is not about doing; it is about being**. It is not how you start but how you finish.

PASSION. PURPOSE. TIME MANAGEMENT.

Allow your
PURPOSE
to become
your
PASSION

Chapter 2
Identifying Calling ("What") vs. Passion ("Why")

Let's face it, if you are free diving 100 feet into the cold ocean, especially in the dark waters off the East coast, you had better be passionate about what you are doing! Kimi laid down her spearfishing career, but from death springs new life! For a moment, her passion for spearfishing fizzled. Finally, she was able to pinpoint concisely why she developed such a hunger for diving. The online publication Mpora writes about Kimi saying, "She began sharing her experiences on social media and gained a whole new following of people who were interest in Kimi's love of the ocean, the environment and living sustainably off the land. People could relate a lot more to that than chasing trophies" she says. "Not only did she not lose her spearfishing career, but she gained new sponsors who cared about her values of eating locally and sustainably too. She became a Patagonia ambassador and now travels the world sharing her environmental messages."[2]

She realized what her true calling was—to educate people about environmental issues concerning the ocean and how to live sustainably. As she learned through personal experience, winning was not her calling neither was being the best diver. She found out what she was created to do. The things that were previously **propelling and driving** her **did not line up with her "what."**

---

[2]   https://mpora.com/diving/meet-hawaiian-spearfisher-swims-great-white-sharks-bites-octopus-brains. Accessed March 23, 2017.

You have a "WHY," but does it line up with your "WHAT?"

After finding her purpose she gained a new love for the ocean and for diving. She now has passion once again for what she laid down because she understands her purpose, her "what." She found her calling which motivated her to pick up her talent of spearfishing with new fervor. Are you ready to find your "what"? Are you ready to stop spinning your wheels in pursuit of things that are not lining up with your calling? I know I am!

NOTES:

PASSION. PURPOSE. TIME MANAGEMENT.

Chapter 3

Why Knowing Your "Why" Is NOT Enough!

I wear many hats in life and I have numerous accomplishments under my belt. However, that didn't stop the constant nagging in my soul that told me that I was missing something deeper, something that was supposed to make a bigger impact for humanity and better utilized my time and talents. I often found it hard to understand how people could lack zeal for what was meaningful in life. After all, I had a passion for so many things that I found it hard to quiet my mind concerning my many projects. Finally, I arrived at a place in life where I realized that **just because I had a passion for something didn't mean that I had a calling in that specific area.**

I will share a very painful story, one I don't share often. I am sharing it with you today because it's part of what brought me to this place in my journey. I am making myself vulnerable and transparent here, so I hope you don't judge me based on what I share. Again, this was a painful experience. I admit that I made many mistakes, but the Father graciously showed me so much after the fact and helped me grow during this process.

For many years, I served as an activist, as "a voice for the voiceless." This sounds like a noble passion, and passionate I was. I worked for humanitarian causes along with hosting a blog that educated my readers about worldwide injustices. I made it my cause to take up the plight and voice of the needy. For years, I dreamed of adopting or fostering kids. I used to look at lists of waiting children and weep for them. I am extremely protective of children, especially my own kids. I understand that we live in a broken world and children are often the victims. Giving my kids an excellent education was not my top motive in homeschooling; instead, we do it because no one will protect them as well as their parents. Because we are so protective I wanted to help as many children and orphans as possible. I even served as a director for a women's and children's shelter for over two years. I wasn't chosen because of my excellent resume but because of my heart to serve. When I came to the shelter, I painted, scrubbed and cleaned. I put my hands to work to show my heart and did what needed to be done. When the position opened up, they asked me to fill it. I prayed about it with my husband and agreed to do it.

NOTES:

PASSION. PURPOSE. TIME MANAGEMENT.

In 2007 with child #4 on my back. I was painting the women's shelter. I always had my kids with me and even they helped to clean and do projects.

At the same time, my husband and I began a two-year international adoption process. However, a timeline of events was about to transpire that would knock the breath right out of us. Before the kids arrived, we faced ongoing trials and struggles, including an undiagnosed illness, causing severe chronic fatigue for my husband. Despite his physical limitations, he continued to work. However, the effects of his exhaustion resulted in a serious accident, and he totaled a vehicle while driving home from work.

My soon to be adopted children were still abroad and had just endured a great earthquake in their country, which accelerated their arrival to the states. On the day of their incoming flight, my only sibling and brother was airlifted to a hospital as his life hung in the balance! As my new children were arriving I was also getting ready to take in my brother's kids as well so that my sister-in-law could be with my brother. I was eight months pregnant and very sick from food intolerance, resulting in chronic headaches and sinus infections. I had severe candida that caused on-going health problems, including terrible fatigue. I was a typically strong woman who could handle much. I actually invited challenges into my life so that I could conquer them. Now, here I stood, physically, mentally, emotionally and even spiritually whipped. Not long after their arrival, all of the kids became very sick as well and life was not getting any easier. A short time later, my brother suffered a severe allergic reaction during surgery, causing him once again to fight for his life. It was so hard because the kids were so new, but I had to drive to the next state to support my brother any way that I could.

Two months later I contracted a virus that was so strong that my vision was blurred for over a month. While I was still sick, I endured a hard and exhausting delivery that was days long. At just eight days old, my infant son was airlifted to a children's hospital after contracting my illness. For the first three or four days in the hospital, the doctors gave him "the million dollar work up" to find out what was wrong with him. He endured endless poking, prodding and dozens of needles. Watching my weak newborn suffer, my heart broke. The pressure nearly pushed me to the breaking point as the strain overwhelmed me.

Additionally, the new children started exhibiting very worrisome behaviors, including inappropriate touching with the other children, acting out toward me and hostility toward the newborn. I felt like such a failure—as if I could not properly protect the children. I started to question if pursuing our "why" meant causing exponential hurt—instead of protection for all. In hindsight, I realize that my thinking was skewed, partially due to my weakened physical state, fear and the trauma of everything that had happened. I felt exhausted and incapable of juggling everything. There is so much that I can't even write about. There was so much stacked against us. I looked in the mirror and thought, "Who are you?" Normally, I stood fiercely even when others fell. Now, I was at my own dead end. At the same time, my marriage was breaking down, and we were in trouble. As if that weren't enough, I was having issues with my extended family. I had never felt more vulnerable and confused. Every morning that I woke up I felt hopeless. I even started thinking that maybe my family would be better off without me, but I knew I had to combat those dark thoughts even though they kept persisting.

One day to momentarily "escape," I went for a run down my long country road. The vivid memory of that day has stayed with me like a snapshot in time. I stopped in the middle of a heavily wooded area, near a rushing creek. Despite the beauty of the day, I was filled with such internal torment and brokenness, I couldn't even enjoy the scenery. I stopped and lifted my hands in the air, loudly crying out with tears streaming down my cheeks. "God, your Word says that I can do all things through you who strengthens me, so why can't I do this? (Philippians 4:13).

I thought you would not give more than I can handle, but I can't handle this. I am so broken. Where are you? I am on…. I then recited my address, once again sobbing, "Where are you?" A gentle breeze blew, and it was as if an audible voice whispered in my ear, **"You can do all things through me, but I have not called you to do all things."** Oh my word! As soon as I heard this, I remembered receiving a word of knowledge from someone two years previously just after we started the adoption process. She did not know about the adoption. She instructed me not to take up someone else's calling because **I would be robbing from the body of believers. Even worse, I would not have the same strength for other tasks as I did when I focused on what I was called to do**.

Immediately, I went into full repentance. I was grieved in my soul. I had been forewarned, and I didn't heed the words because I was blinded—**blinded by the drive of my passion** to protect the unprotected. I always knew my "why" and reason for doing things, **but I missed an important factor that superseded my "why."** If someone would have asked me, "Why do you do what you do?" I had an immediate response—to take up the cause of the needy and to be a voice for the voiceless so that the oppressed can go free. My reasons were solid, but I was missing my "what." **"Knowing my what" is defined as knowing and understanding what purpose <u>I was created to fulfill</u> in life.** The same is true for you. **"Knowing your what"** means that you know your purpose in life and **why you were created.**

Could your PASSION be blinding you?

Uncover your CALLING!

That day on the country road, I repented for not realizing that I was trying to operate in another person's calling. I was at a low place in my life and felt like the ultimate failure. To add insult to injury, people said and did incredibly cruel things during that time. My isolation overwhelmed me. I was not operating in strength but in weakness and in sparsity. **Why do some people seem to succeed** in their life experiences while some do not? I believe the reason is this: **some people were called, and some were not.**

I have interviewed countless adoptive parents over the years. A friend told me that one of her adopted daughters slammed her head into a kitchen cabinet. However, she saw it as a challenge, and she likes challenges! She shared other stories of what she went through and I soon realized that she had extra grace for such situations because it was her calling to adopt. Did you hear that? You have EXTRA grace given to YOU in your area of calling. When you try to walk in someone else's calling, the extra measure might not be available to you to such a degree! What I am sharing with you now still brings a deep reverential fear and great humility to me when I think of it.We also learned that my husband was operating out of a place of past hurts in his decision making. In our prayer time we learned why we veered from our personal calling. **My husband has his own personal testimony about this time in our life.** As for me, my activism and frustration with the mistreatment of children was propelled by my frustration with God. He showed me tht I wanted to take up this cause because I felt like He wasn't doing enough to protect children. So, I was going to help Him and make it my cause to be a voice where I felt He was being silent. I was so humbled when I heard this. I was so broken. I was put in my place as my motives were revealed to me.

My "why" was misguided, so it didn't line up with my "what." I now realize my "what" comes from above; my divine assignment and my "why" comes from within.
<u>NOTES:</u>

My "WHAT" comes from ABOVE. My "WHY" comes from within.

I still care about the needs of hurting children, but how I go about helping them is now in line with my life's purpose and what I was created to do. I understand that I can help them in other ways and still remain in step with my calling. I am much more fulfilled because everything is in balance and done with the right heart and not from a place of hurt or mistrust.

We are all created with a unique calling, a unique purpose. **I now "know my what" and what I was born to do**. I was created to be fierce in the kingdom and to stand upon truth and to inspire others to walk in their life's purpose. I was created to mother and bear children who will become future world changers because of the message I have poured into them over their lives. Sixteen years ago, I heard something similar to this in my prayer time. "You will impact many women on a broader scale for My sake." I journaled that paraphrased entry but forgot about it for years. **I was created to make an impact and to have a voice that will inspire others to live out their highest calling.** That is why this book was born. Knowing my life's purpose doesn't mean that I don't get off track as I pursue 101 passions, some of which work toward my calling and others that detract from it. I only succeed and find peace when I reevaluate my projects in the light of my calling. Ask yourself and pray as you do some serious soul searching then ask yourself the following questions below:

- What propels my passions?
- Why do I do what I do?
- Am I lead by fear or by the accolades of man?
- Do I operate based upon past hurts or unfulfilled needs?
- Do I understand my "what" so that it can propel my "why?"

Understanding your "what" will keep your "why" on point with your calling.

NOTES:

Chapter 4
Uniquely You

Our society is overly obsessed with stars, athletes and the rich and famous, while suffering from a void of uniqueness. Everyone is trying to look like her, talk and walk like him, trying to play like them. Where is the uniqueness in our culture? Where is the desire to be original? If you are searching for your calling you have to start with accepting how God created you. There is so much written on self-love and in some cases there is a lot to be learned from this topic. Show me a man or woman who is unhappy with themselves and I can almost guarantee they will be unhappy with everyone else around them! Society is so conflicted it seems, so many people want to stand out from the crowd, but they are doing everything they can to be clones of someone else. What if everyone truly desired to be genuine and stopped trying to act like someone else? What would that look like? The lure of tabloids and plastic surgery would diminish. The commercial industry would be in an uproar, no longer able to entice the masses. They would lose their power to seduce people into wanting perfection wrapped up in the latest and greatest brands. Instead, people would understand that they don't "need" this or that to be a better or more attractive person. The world as we know it would turn upside down! Can you imagine it? The puppet strings would be cut.

As a society, we have lost our flavor—the flavor of our

uniqueness. Instead, imagine a world where everyone knew their purpose and was not interested in being somebody other than who they were created to be. We are all guilty; we have all fallen short in this area. Why is this? Because as soon as we enter this world, we are bombarded with messages shouting at us to covet what we don't have. This is on top of the fact that within us, we often desire things that are forbidden. Think of Eve in the garden and how she longed for the forbidden fruit. The societal machine just feeds that desire. There are always those who tell us we will never be good enough, strong enough or smart enough. Of course, most of the time they will offer a solution that was manufactured in dark places. Now, imagine if you were only interested in being you. Imagine if you were no longer fighting to be what the world says you should be. **How high could you rise? How would you impact the world by giving the very best of the unique you?** What if you laid down the weight of comparison and looked at who God created you to be since the beginning of time? You can't make other people change, but you can change **you**! Now, imagine if tens, then hundreds, then thousands, and on and on adopted a new way and chose to be unique. How productive, **whole** and balanced would our world be? If there is one thing I have learned over and over, it is this, **"You can't control what others do, but you can control what you do." It starts with you—in your mind and in your heart.** When you can stand by personal convictions, when you can stand above reproach because you know that you are continually giving your best and staying true to your calling, then you can stand with dignity and perseverance without being derailed from your goals even when the haters and the seducers come your way.

PASSION. PURPOSE. TIME MANAGEMENT.

UNIQUELY YOU!

"Before I formed you in the womb I knew you, before you were born I set you apart." Jer. 1:5 NIV

Use this page to write out your own personal meme, impact statement or draw a picture. Get creative. Come back to it to ENCOURAGE yourself.

I have to admit that as I wrote this chapter, I almost searched to see what other authors were saying on this topic, but I caught myself and stopped. I made a personal stand to remain true to this message and declared, "No. I will be unique in this area. I don't need to be inspired by others to write about something I know I have within me. I have my own message, my own perspective. I don't need to see what others are saying on what I have been called to write about." So, I stopped, and I prayed, "Father give me charisma (grace/Spirit empowerment) to write about what you have called me to." Do you know that it doesn't matter if this book makes it to the top 100? No, if I touch just one person, if I impact one life for the better and for the Kingdom, then I have accomplished my goal in writing it. I believe in the **power of one!** I understand that it only takes one impacted individual to change the course of history as we know it.

I will never forget the story of William Wilberforce, born in 1759. As a young man, he saw the act of the day, slave trading, as wicked. He was just one man, persecuted for his beliefs, but his name went down in the annals of time for persisting in his fight against the abolition of slavery. He was just a single man, but he made a great impact on history with his determination and heed to his calling.[3]

A section in my family blog states, "Don't live for applause, live for a cause!" Can you imagine how much better the world would be if everyone lived this way? Now imagine if you lived this way. How would your life change? How would you impact

---

3
http://www.bbc.co.uk/history/historic_figures/wilberforce_william.shtml. Accessed March 22, 2017.

the world? Change begins with you!

NOTES:

Don't live
for
applause,
LIVE
for
a
CAUSE!

Prayer:

Father, I thank You that I am fearfully and wonderfully made. You knew me while I was yet in my mother's womb; You knew me and formed me (Psalm 139). You created me, unique and in Your image so that I would be complete in You. Help me not to live for applause but to live for a cause. Help me to **run the race of life with passion, purpose and uniqueness.** Amen.

<u>NOTES:</u>

Chapter 5
4 Steps to Find Your Calling—Your "What"

1. Pray and seek the answer in Scripture
2. Examine your passions
3. Listen to your life
4. Create a personal mission statement

Step 1-Pray and seek the answer in Scripture

I am sure many of you have prayed constantly about finding your calling only to end up with no solid answers. However, I encourage you to search the Scriptures to find truths and principles to stand on.

"I, therefore, the prisoner of the Lord, beseech you to walk (conduct your life) worthy of the calling (a divine call) with which you were called (summoned)" Ephesians 4:1 (NKJV)[4]

"Take a good look, friends, at who you were when you got called into this life. I don't see many of "the brightest and the best" among you, not many influential, not many from high-society families. Isn't it obvious that God deliberately chose

---

4

http://www.godrules.net/library/kjvstrongs/kjvstrongseph4.htm. Accessed March 22, 2017,

men and women that the culture overlooks and exploits and abuses, chose these "nobodies" to expose the hollow pretensions of the "somebodies?" That makes it quite clear that none of you can get by with blowing your own horn before God. Everything that we have—right thinking and right living, a clean slate and a fresh start—comes from God by way of Jesus Christ" 1 Corinthians 1:26 (The Message).

When I think of the men and women in the Bible that were handed their calling, I envision people working at their daily occupations, suddenly whisked away to fulfill their destiny. King David was just a shepherd boy, the youngest of his brothers. He was not expecting anything grand for his life, yet he was **called** as a king and a ruler. He was plucked out of the mundane and thrust into greatness! Likewise, the disciples stepped away from the daily grind of their occupations to answer their call to step into their destiny! How exciting does that sound? Who doesn't want to leave behind the dullness of daily life to step into a world of excitement, filled with hope? I know that I would love to feel that excitement at the end of every day.

According to the Wall Street Journal, in 2014, less than 30 percent of workers globally felt "very satisfied" with their occupations.[5] What does that tell you about the frustration most people must feel every day?

You might say, "Yes, but those people in the Bible were minding their own business when they received their calling. Why haven't I heard anything specific for my life?" This is a

---

5
    http://blogs.wsj.com/atwork/2014/06/18/u-s-workers-cant-get-no-job-satisfaction/ Accessed March 22, 2017.

very valid question. The answer is found when you look further back into their lives. For example, what positioned David, a lowly shepherd boy, for such a high calling? While still a youth, David exhibited inner fortitude and took his job seriously as a shepherd boy. He protected the sheep with his life, battling bears and lions to safeguard the flock. When he was about 15, he battled a giant named Goliath and won (See I Samuel 15). He won because he was fearless, strategic, and most of all, he trusted God to help him defeat his opponent. So while it seems strange that a shepherd boy, the least of his brothers, would be called to be a king, we can see in hindsight that he was moving in his calling even while he was still in the field of the mundane.

One who is faithful in a very little will also be faithful in much, according to Luke 16:10 KJV

Since not everyone has such a spirited start in life, the greater concern and question is this, "Are you being faithful and diligent even in the mundane? Are you treating this season of your life as if your future depends on it? Are you being faithful with the little so that you will be faithful with the much?"

Take time to answer the above questions now:

_____

_____

_____

Has your view of your current circumstances been skewed? How?

_____

_____

How can you have a better attitude? How can you be more diligent?

_____

_____

In your time of reflection, remember the great news, "For the gifts and the calling of God are irrevocable" Romans 11:29. Our calling in life was established long before we could even utter a single word.

Another version says it this way,

"God's gifts and God's call are under full warranty—never canceled, never rescinded" (The Message Bible).

The pre-eminent questions are these:

Are you going to waste your life doing what you weren't called to do?

or

Will you instead listen to the still, small voice, saying, "This is the way, walk in it?" Isaiah 30:21 (NKJV)

Have you become so focused on finances that your thoughts are clouded with only generating money?

Scripture says, "Before I formed you in the womb I knew you; before you were born I sanctified you; I *ordained* you..." Jeremiah 1:5 (Paraphrase of the KJV).

Honestly, I can only assume that although the gifts and the calling are irrevocable, we can actually choose to ignore them! **We can choose to pursue things apart from our calling and forfeit the great satisfaction that comes from doing what we are created to do. Remember pursuits can be exciting and still leave you feeling completely empty if you are not called to do them.** So many occupations are available in life from the mundane to the great. Some people work in the mundane, totally satisfied because they are doing what they are meant to do. Others seem to walk in greatness but are emotionally and spiritually empty because they have missed their true calling.

NOTES:

Pursuits can be **EXCITING** and still leave you feeling completely empty if you are **NOT** called to do them.

I cannot emphasis this enough: status and wealth do not fulfill a person; knowing why you were created—knowing your "what" and walking in that purpose does. Remember, you were created with a purpose. Even while you were knit in your mother's womb, you had an assignment for your life. Your life counts; it has meaning; it is supposed to positively impact others. Mother Theresa was not seeking fortune and fame or looking to achieve greatness. Following her call birthed a passion in her heart, recognized around the globe. She didn't ask for accolades but received them anyway as she became known around the world. Her name will not soon be forgotten even though she has now left this earth. She followed her calling, becoming a servant to hurting children who really needed her love and support. She found her great reward in living out her purpose.

Prayer:

Father, hear my heart. I desire to know my calling so that I may walk in it. Show me my blind spots and prune me so that I might bear new fruit. Show me anything that is hindering me from my calling. Make me worthy of my destiny. Guard my eyes, my heart and my mind. Bind the enemy from not allowing me to hear your still, small voice as you guide me. Let me walk in greatness by your Spirit so that I can live an amazing life. Amen.

Step 2-Examine your passions

In this step, we will focus on the "obvious for some" and "not so obvious" for others. As I mentioned earlier, I am a woman full of many passions. I have so many passions that I sometimes feel overwhelmed with too many exciting options to pursue. However, some people feel really clueless about what drives them or what brings them true fulfillment in life.

Those with many passions struggle to understand how an individual cannot have any idea about what spells out p-a-s-s-i-o-n for them. This is where relational value comes into play. I will address both issues, but remember the other point of view in this chapter. When we understand why other people do what they do, we can gain more insight to their actions. This allows us to become effective counselors when so many feel lost. Many times, people don't even have answers for themselves, let alone for others.

First point of view- "I know what I am passionate about."

I definitely fit into this category. When I look back at my life, various forms of activism have clearly driven me. I have always been passionate about being a voice for those who could not stand on their own. I am passionate about creating community and stirring up others to take action. As a senior in high school, I was nominated to be the liaison for Students Rights and Responsibilities. I am 42 years old as I write this book. I was already drawn to a platform to stand for others even 25 years ago. As I grew older, I became very active in various women's functions and ministries. I served as a hospitality coordinator for a monthly women's conference, a conference speaker, prayer leader, and as a director for a women's and children's recovery home for more than two years. My philosophy has always been, **"Don't complain about problems, be an answer to them."** As soon as I found myself complaining about something, in the next breath, I brainstormed how I could bring a solution to the problem.

In 2003, I became extremely ill. After many failed attempts by doctors to figure out what was wrong with me, I went on a full hunt to find out the problem for myself. I discovered that gluten and candida were upsetting my system. At the time, you could not find quality gluten-free (GF) products, and GF bread tasted like cardboard. I had a choice to complain about my options or to create a solution. I did not know how to bake gluten-free; my creations were barely palatable. However, I prayed, "Father, teach me how to bake gluten-free so that I can bless others. Father, I know how people feel when they can't enjoy their food—when they can't enjoy life!—any longer." To my excitement, my prayers were answered! In 2011, I opened up a licensed home bakery called, "Sweets You Can Eat." Our mantra was, "Have your cake and eat it, too!" I adopted this slogan because I personally felt the pain of serving cake that I could not even eat at many of my own parties. In 2013, we grew out of our former name, changing it to "Compelled Bakery," as we became progressive in our mission. Our slogan emerged as "a gluten-free bakery with a cause." Now our baked goods have been flown around the USA and featured at popular restaurants! I became a solution to my greatest problem and stayed true to my convictions.

I am passionate about always remaining true to myself and being a leader rather than a follower. I am empowered when I am the only who one will stand. I don't mind being the odd ball out or the one that looks different from everyone else. Personally, I do not bow to popular opinion and I am only driven by personal convictions. I find this rewarding and empowering.

These motives might not seem to need deep scrutiny. However, **I have learned that even our best intentions must be scrutinized.** As the saying goes, "My greatest is strength is also my greatest weakness." I challenged myself with this thought in 2012 as I mentioned earlier. I questioned my passions and my motives and was completely humbled during the process. I had come to the end of myself and found myself wanting.

I was deflated and then changed in the twinkling of an eye. I am serious! I went by Emma my whole life, but by the time I dug to the root of my thinking, I wanted to only be called EmmaSara. I wanted Emma to die. Why? Why was I so affected by what happened on the end of that street so many years ago? It was because the Father had exposed my heart and showed me a **huge** blind spot. He revealed why I was so passionate and strong about this particular cause—my passion was propelled by **fear**!

Fear is not of the Father.

"For God has not given us a spirit of fear, but of power and of love and of a sound mind" 2 Timothy 1:7 (KJV).

If I was propelled by something that was not of the Father, I needed to examine why I was doing what I was doing. The Spirit answered, "You do not trust that I am taking care of the situation. You thought you would nobly take up the cause where I was lacking!" Ouch! My heart was crushed as I listened to what was really in my soul. I didn't see it with my human mind, but my spirit was suddenly agreeing with what I was hearing, and I could not hide from the truth! I—along with my motives—was uncovered.

I repented for my pride, for my distrust, for my fear. Once I did, I was able to move forward into my **true** calling.

Second point of view- "I'm not sure what I'm passionate about."

In this second area, many of you lack passion for much of anything. Sure, you might do things that bring you momentary pleasure, and you might not even have a problem jumping on board with someone else's passion. However, you have a deficit in this area for yourself. You might even have a hard time pinpointing anything significant that motivates you. Even though I didn't have an issue with this, many people that are close to me suffer from passionless lives. Maybe you do as well. Some days, this might seem like a disease that eats at your soul as you roam aimlessly through life, helping others fulfill their pursuits while you have no clear drive or goal to aim for. Don't get me wrong—these people can be hard workers, focused, and even be involved in causes. However, their true colors will eventually show through, if not to others, then to themselves. **The fruit will show the root.** A person who has a true passion for something will seldom allow it to die or deflate when something doesn't go their way. People without passion will move full steam ahead, doing something that seems pleasurable to them, only to hit a bump in the road and decide that perhaps this passion isn't worth pursuing after all.. Like the proverbial stone thrown at a glass house, it quickly cracks and is destroyed. People who lack passion commonly suffer from depression. Further investigation into this area reveals other root problems as well. Just like my own roots and reasons needed to be unearthed, so does the root of the person who lacks the fire of passion.

While every human is truly unique, the works of satan are not. He plots and plans to bring the same kind of destruction to everyone—to kill, steal, and destroy. He loves to steal a person's identity in Christ. He enjoys robbing individuals of self-esteem and destroying dreams that bring hope. Another common aspect to this "dis-ease" of the soul is lack of identity in Christ or, in other words, who you are in Him and **who you were created to be**. When you don't know your identity or why you were created, then you will be tempted to base your identity on who others want you to be. This creates a recipe for disaster since we will never be able to fulfill every person's expectations for us. Sooner or later, we will let them down, and when we do, the root will be exposed, unveiling our motives. Unfortunately, some people are so wrapped up in the pain of failure that they can't see their own issues, a personal defect. They will be too busy licking their wounds and rehearsing their pain to view the fact that their heart was not in the right place to begin with. When we do something for others for our own personal gain, whether financial, verbal, emotional or otherwise, we are not acting from a pure motive but from a selfish motive. Let's face it, many people operate this way. You will know you are operating from selfish gain or a victim spirit if your glass house shatters when you are not acknowledged for your work or if you crumble under possibly warranted negative criticism.

Conversely, the select few who do things from a pure and giving heart expect nothing in return, not a thanks, not a pat on the back, not a raise. They do a kind deed just to bless others without any need for repayment. Those are the people who have true contentment in life.

Uncovering each of these areas of personal defect is truly a difficult nut to crack. I have yet to talk to a person who is operating in a broken area of their life who actually **knows** they are broken. As I stated, I moved in strength and in passion, accomplishing much for the first 39 years of my life, but I was broken. The entire time, **I was operating and moving in super strength, out of fear.** It is so true that many of the world's strongest people are actually the weakest; they just know how to cover their fears more effectively. For people who lack vision or passion, I highly suggest that you read the upcoming books in my Compelled Lifestyle Series. This area is one where many of us surely need deliverance, and this series will pique your interest. I will give you powerful tools to defeat this defective mindset. If this is speaking to you, I pray that you receive a miracle and change your mindset today! However, if you are still stuck, sign up for our mailing list at www.emmasara.com or email me at compelledlife@gmail.com, and we will notify you when my books are released!

Self-Reflect

Take the time to answer these questions. Be honest with yourself.
Are you a people pleaser? _____

_____

_____

If you don't know, answer the following question: Do you decide what to do based on the approval or disapproval of others? _____

Are you driven by the accolades of men?_____

_____

Put another way, are you driven by success, or do you need to be in the lime light?

_____

_____

Are you operating out of fear?
_____
_____

Are you still unsatisfied after pursuing what you thought were your passions?_____
_____
_____

If you answered "yes" to any of the above, you need to take a personal moral inventory. This takes time as you intentionally set aside a season to let the Holy Spirit speak to you about areas of weakness in your life. If you continue operating from the wrong motives, you will never walk in peace and fulfillment even if you find your purpose and calling in life.
Prayer- Examine your motives

Father, you know my heart and my blind spots. Reveal my innermost motives to me. Show me why I am driven in certain areas. Show me if my drive is propelled from a broken place in my life. Father, lead me in a path of righteousness and let all I do flow from a teachable heart. Let me have pure motives and allow me to operate from a place of true strength rather than weakness. Amen.

Step 3-Listen to Your Life

Now comes the fun part of assessing your life's calling. Every day on earth, our life has been speaking to us. Whether yelling or whispering, it is speaking. This is the time to self-reflect and think about your daily life.

This time, we will start with a prayer so that your mind is clear as you answer the following questions.

Father, Please help me to respond honestly to the following questions. Help me pinpoint my purpose. Let my answers lead me to a deeper understanding of my life's calling. Amen.

Additional Prayer:

LISTEN TO YOUR LIFE!

Every day on earth, our life has been speaking to us. Whether yelling or whispering, it is speaking. What is it saying to you?

Use this page to write out your own personal meme, impact statement or draw a picture. Get creative. Come back to it to ENCOURAGE yourself.

We were granted permission to utilize this set of six questions from "Christianity Today." "**Discovering your God-given Calling**" by Julia Mateer, Feb. 7, 2013, These questions will help you dig deep to find answers. Take a moment to consider the following questions:

1. If money were not an issue, what would you do with your time?

_____
_____
_____
_____

2. What do you love to do? What do you hate to do?

_____
_____
_____
_____

3. What gives you energy? What drains the life out of you?

_____
_____
_____
_____

4. What do you want to change, shape, and leave better than you found it?

_____
_____
_____
_____

5. What segment of the population are you drawn to help?

_____
_____
_____

6. What do you want to experience, witness, and learn?

_____
_____
_____

7. After answering these questions do you see any kind of patterns emerging in your life? What is your life saying to you?

_____
_____
_____

8. How do your answers line up with your current situation or occupation?[6]

_____
_____
_____
_____

---

[6] http://www.christianitytoday.com/women-leaders/2013/february/discover-your-god-given-calling.html. Accessed March 22, 2017.

As I thought about this comprehensive list, I came up with a few more ideas to help you dig deep into your purpose. Take the time to ask those who are closest to you to give you a list of qualities they value about you. Tell them about your quest to find your purpose. Ask them to share any insights they might have with you. Ask them what they see as your greatest strengths and weaknesses.

What did you learn from your interviews?

_____
_____
_____
_____
_____

What insight surprised you the most?

_____
_____
_____
_____
_____

LISTEN TO YOUR LIFE!

Every day on earth, our life has been speaking to us. Whether yelling or whispering, it is speaking. What is it saying to you?

Use this page to write out your own personal meme, impact statement or draw a picture. Get creative. Come back to it to ENCOURAGE yourself.

You should now have a closer blueprint to the burning question about your purpose and calling. You should begin to have a better idea of the direction that you need to take. I recommend reviewing this chapter annually to do a self-evaluation and make sure you are on the right track to pursuing goals with lasting value.

Step 4- Create a Personal Mission Statement

This is the chapter you will return to over and over again **because this is where you will write your own chapter.** Even if you leave this book to continue to search for your specific calling, one thing is for certain: if you complete this chapter, you will have a blueprint for life! This blueprint will allow you to easily make decisions about business offers. It will allow you to weed through and eliminate many **good** projects so that you can choose the **best** projects.

Did you know that the enemy of the best is the good? As the saying goes, **if satan can't make you bad, he will make you busy**. We don't want to spin our wheels with endless good projects that drain the life and resources out of us. However, if we have a strong mission statement, we will only accept the best projects that bring us closer to our goals—those that line up with our mission statement and that give us great satisfaction at the end of the day. Who doesn't want to feel greatly satisfied? Remember, if you would like to create a dynamic and impacting mission statement, write it out and put it where you can see it.

MY MISSION STATEMENT
I live my life with a purpose. I have a standard. I have a focus!

_____
_____
_____

Use this page to write out your own mission statement. Then, utilize this section for visual inspiration and creativity. Come back and feast on your food for thought.

You should feel pumped when you recite it. You should feel motivated when you read it. You don't want it to sound like eloquent mumbo jumbo. It needs to have **power** for **your** life. It needs to speak to your inner being and **pull**, not push, you to achieve personal growth. It shouldn't be so vague that its statement could be for anyone. This has to be a mission statement for you or, if you are married, for your family. It has to be a foundation that you will stand upon when making any and all future decisions. It has to be somewhat instructive and reveal character. It must speak with resolve. The most effective mission statement can be drafted in a paragraph, and you should be able to read it in 30 seconds or less, or it will not meet your immediate need. It needs to be strong enough to help to steer you and short enough to recite at the drop of a hat. If it's too long, you will struggle to memorize it. Your statement will be your anchor—the anchor that you and your family need—to keep you from drifting away from your long-term goals.

Creating Your Mission Statement
Details: Make it clear, memorable, and concise. Instead of specific rules about the length of a mission statement, remember that you can pack more of a punch into fewer words.

Remember, your mission statement should do the following:
- Encompass the values that drive your personal or business transactions.
- Reflect your personality,
- Explain how you will treat others, and

Address how you want others to see you or your brand.

Common outline terms for building a strong statement are:
- **Who?**
- **What?**
- **How?**
- **Whom?** This also addresses "given value" or to whom you will be an asset.

Use colorful, powerful words that evoke passion when you read your statement. For example, strong verbs encourage specific action instead of passivity. You should feel like you just stopped in and filled up your nearly empty gas tank. Your mission statement should set you ablaze with an internal fire, driving you toward your destiny. When other people hear it, they should become excited about what you have to offer. A post from Kinesis, Inc. worded it wonderfully.

"When you live your mission through your business brand, then amazing, phenomenal things start to happen. Your perfect, dream clients are drawn to you. People get really excited about what you are doing. They spread the word to their friends, they sign up for your services, they give you great testimonials. You get more customers, make more revenue, and your business grows with ease. And best of all – your team is more creative and having more fun than ever before because everyone is in absolute alignment with your *Why*." - Wendy Maynard, July 10, 2010.[7]

When our family was creating our mission statement, we wanted to work on it as a team. My husband put together a

---

[7] https://www.kinesisinc.com/how-to-write-a-powerful-mission-statement/. Accessed March 22, 2017,

complete slide show and presentation that encompassed our family's long-term goals. As his wife, it really helped me to see his ideas come to life on the screen. In life, we all have our strengths and weaknesses. If you ever research highly effective people, you will find that they understand their own weaknesses, so they surround themselves with people who are strong in the areas that they are not. **We need to learn to maximize our strengths and delegate our weaknesses.**[8]

My husband gave a great presentation. We discussed the vision together and went to work, contributing as a whole to create ownership of it. Collaboration can prove challenging if you do not have a humble heart. Pride can be your biggest roadblock to achieving great successes in life. My husband realized that a lot was at stake if we didn't get it right. Therefore, he was open to creating a family mission statement written by all of us together. I will walk you through the creative process step by step that went into drafting our mission statement.

The original mission statement:
#1 "The McMillions are a legacy of world changers that submit to Yeshua's righteous beacon of hope."

Note: Yeshua is the Hebrew name for Jesus. We agreed that we could easily memorize this since it was short. However, this statement lacked some key elements. Let's look at the details.
Who? The McMillions

---

[8] http://www.howardfarran.com/howard-speaks/focus-on-your-strengths-delegate-your-weaknesses/. Accessed March 22, 2017.

What? World changers
How? Submit to Yeshua's righteous beacon of hope.
Whom? The kids were having a hard time identifying this area.

The focus for each question encompasses the following:

Who? This is an identity statement
What? What you aim to accomplish or your specific purpose.
How? How to accomplish your mission
Whom? The people you are going to affect
After reviewing the first draft, we made the following revisions:

Draft #2 We are a generation of leaders that brings hope and inspiration to the multitudes. We operate with integrity and high energy to leave a legacy of world changers by the power of Christ.

Draft #3 We are a generation of leaders focused on creating a legacy of hope to inspire the multitudes. We operate with integrity and high energy.

Draft #4 We are generation of leaders focused on creating a legacy of world changers that bring hope to inspire the multitudes. We operate with integrity and high energy.

Drafts #1 through #4 all had the same problem: While we are clear about our identity and what we want to accomplish, we do not state **how** we plan to achieve that goal.

Finally, we found our keeper on the fifth try. After reviewing all of our drafts, we agreed on this last statement. In the process, we kept having the kids recite each one out loud and asked them how it made them feel, what they remembered and if they felt it could be improved upon. This was our final result.

Final #5
The McMillions are a generation of leaders focused on creating a legacy of world changers. We are ambassadors of Christ who work with integrity and high energy to inspire others by sharing powerful tools for life.

After we wrote this final draft, we asked ourselves the four foundational questions:

Who? Our identity—we are leaders and ambassadors for Christ.
What? We are creating a legacy of world changers.
How? By inspiring and sharing powerful tools for life.
Whom? We are changing the world or those in our sphere of influence.

Now, let's review the original draft and statement.
#1 "The McMillions are a legacy of world changers that submit to Yeshua's righteous beacon of hope."
Who? The McMillions
What? World changers
How? Submit to Yeshua's righteous beacon of hope.
Whom? Here is where the original draft fell short. We did not have a strong whom.

While the first draft was a start, we did not feel that it was a strong mission statement to anchor our family. We didn't sense that it could be used as an avenue to help us prioritize or reject projects.

On the other hand, by our fifth try, we felt we understood our identity statement, what we were supposed to do and how we were supposed to do it.

This is the foundation of a mission statement. If it does not contain a strategy or the ability to motivate you, just keep working on it until it contains all those elements.
We also drafted a family decree.

We have seven kids, and we really want to sow virtue and integrity into them using every means possible. We decided to make a decree because we saw the power of having one in the biblical story of the Rechabites in Jeremiah 35. The father in this family established a family decree that passed down from generation to generation. When the entire family faced a challenging situation, they recited the family decree as a standard that they lived by. This family has gone down in the annals of time for following the creed of their forefathers and their ancestors. The Lord saw their dedication and commitment and honored them for it.

McMillion Creed and Affirmations

1. We submit our life to Yeshua's will.
2. We are messengers of Yeshua's hope.
3. We take initiative to advance the Kingdom.
4. We are world changers with a generational mindset.
5. We do not love the world or the things in the world.
6. We love correction because we love wisdom.
7. We make calculated decisions based upon prayer, the Word and our decision protocol.

I cover the decision protocol in the accompanying workbook to "Passion. Purpose. Time Management." due out by January 2018. Prepare to dive into deeper waters as you explore the in-depth contents of this book.

Mission Statement Worksheet

For your first draft, don't overthink it too much. Just write down the first thing that comes to mind as a possible statement.
Draft #1

_____
_____
_____

From this draft, develop the following areas:

Who? (Your identity statement)_____
What?_____
How? _____
Whom? (Your audience)_____

Next, find a piece of paper and start working on your mission statement. When you finish your final draft, come back and document it in your book to mark the start of your journey.

Final Draft - Date_____

_____
_____

Whenever you hit a snag as you make decisions, come back to your final draft and ask yourself if the possible project lines up with your mission statement. Answer honestly. Don't forget to include other people in the process to help you with any blind spots you might have. According to Proverbs 11:14, there is wisdom in a multitude of counselors.

NOTES:

Chapter 6
Making Time Deliver

In 1716, Christopher Bullock stated in the "Cobler of Preston," " 'Tis impossible to be sure of anything but Death and Taxes."[9] However, as a mother of seven children, I can add to that list! It is seems that there are always fewer hours in the day than necessary to accomplish all that I would like to do! You can have a legit mission statement and understand your calling, but if you squander away your time on "good things," you will undoubtedly end up frustrated and feeling defeated. As I mentioned earlier, "The enemy of the best is the good, and if satan can't make you bad, he will make you busy with a lot of good things."

Did you know that satan can be creative? **It is true that he can even inspire you to do great things.** You might wonder how that is possible. While it is true that satan has nothing good in him, the initial work can be as problematic as the final outcome. If he can divert you from the path God has for you in hopes that you will take the bait and be filled with pride, greed, or worse, then he is comfortable sharing "good" ideas with you. **He loves to derail people from God's best. For this reason, it's imperative that you not only choose your**

---

9   http://www.nytimes.com/2008/07/21/magazine/27wwwl-guestsafire-t.html. Accessed March 22, 2017.

projects carefully, but that you also fiercely protect your time so that you can live a life of purpose. In the next chapter, we will discuss ways to protect your time.

NOTES:

Chapter 7

Protecting Your Time

Step 1 Create a Schedule

In the following three chapters I am going to discuss 3-steps to protect your time.

1. Create a Schedule
2. Create Goals
3. Create Safeguards

Let's start with step one: creating a schedule to protect your time. As I think about the topic of scheduling, I can almost see the tug of war in my mind between the two camps. The pro-schedule side might think, "Scheduling isn't new to me. It's is effective, if I stick to it." While the anti-schedule side might say, "I loathe scheduling! It's too restrictive and stresses me out!" To each camp, I would reply that both of your views hold truth. At the end of the day, a schedule is only as effective as you allow it to be. **If we create a schedule and then allow sabotage to come in and rob us of time, our schedule becomes nothing more than a list of good ideas.** We must implement the schedule as much as possible throughout the day. If an unexpected event happens, roll with the punches and then jump back on track and continue on!

Sometimes, we have to remind ourselves why scheduling is important. First, it creates a sense of order. **God is a God of order. He is the ultimate scheduler.**

YAHWEH is a God of order & the Ultimate Scheduler

After all, the stars, the sun, and the moon all function according to a set schedule. They show their glory at just the right time of the day, every day. Plants and wildlife flourish beautifully according to seasons, all on nature's schedule. If we run from schedules, we are sure to hit disorder and/or chaos at some point. I am not saying that I always use a schedule. However, when I do, I love it because my days run more efficiently. When I don't use a schedule, our life shows the fruit, not just in our immediate household, but to those around us as well. Disorder can cause chaos, which is hard to hide.

NOTES:

Married 2 years. I was a young bride who was eager to grow.

One of my favorite examples of this is from my early years of marriage. I was a young bride, and my husband was even younger. He was only 21 with less than two years in the military and low seniority. Our small base housed about 300 service personnel. My husband was a focused young man but didn't know how to plan. As a new bride, I was eager to gain tools on how to be successful in life and in marriage. I began to read books on time management, and I decided we both could improve in this area. To help us, I ordered us both day planners. He was less than enthused about using his and dragged his feet when it came time to use it. I really had to sell him on the idea of using it. Each time he forgot an appointment, I nonchalantly mentioned that his planner could help him remember important dates and lists. At some point, he realized that trying to mentally remember information was stressing him out. He picked up his planner and started to fill it in, and before I knew it, he was taking it to work. Here he was, at just 21, becoming highly effective because he was using a new tool. Before this, he was extremely forgetful. As a matter of fact, he still is! However, during this season, he began to gain a reputation in his department at work as someone who was organized and on top of what was going on. He started using his planner to take notes, write down dates, and keep to-do lists at home and work. He became extremely dependable on the job. Before I knew it, he was put into a position of leadership way above his rank, which is not typical in the military. They were short staffed, but my husband was showing himself approved and became self-qualified.

Over the years, I have watched him set his planner aside. Doing so resulted in stress, confusion and frustration. To be honest, we both have seen the same poor fruit when we did not use a planner. Notice I said, "use." We have had planners for the past two years, but having a planner is not the same as consistently using one. Scheduling and planning only produce notable fruit if they are used consistently. A month ago, my husband found his old day planner in storage. He pulled it out and dusted it off. He ordered new inserts for it and began using it again. He has tried using lists and a different book planner over the past year, but they didn't really work for him. I asked him about the difference between using the original planner and trying new systems, and he responded, "This planner is the only planner that has given me consistent results. I am ready to use it again." I noted that he liked this planner because it was in a ring-binder format, and he could add to it annually. That meant that he didn't have to buy a new planner each year. Instead, he can just take out sections he doesn't need and keep sections he wants from year to year. This provides him with consistency. I really laugh when I remember his first remarks about scheduling and planning and how he thought they were stressful. Just the thought of using them made him cringe visibly. Now here he was, almost 20 years later, with a completely different mindset.

More often than not, we have to be willing to step out of our comfort zone to accomplish great things. With a family of nine and with homeschooling, life can be complicated and unpredictable. Many days, such a detailed schedule of tasks seems impossible. Instead, I started using blocks of time rather than specific times. I put four specific times on my schedule as a point of reference. For me, those are waking up and meal times—breakfast, lunch and dinner. Next, I created time blocks that worked around those pre-set times to accomplish necessary tasks throughout the day. Everyone really liked this better than having a detailed time list. They said that "they felt less hurried or stressed when something unexpected happened during the day." They felt that time blocks gave them more time and flexibility to accomplish what they needed to do.

Here is an example from a past schedule. Our life is very fluid and unpredictable. As such, my time blocks adjust to match our needs each week. I do not account for every hour in the day. Instead, I focus on accomplishing each task within that specific time frame before the day ends.

Time Block Schedule

6 a.m. Wake up/Bible morning routine

Two hrs. Homework or book work

9 a.m. Breakfast

10 a.m. School starts for kids

Time Blocks

30 min. Teach younger kids

30 min. Chores

30 min. Prepare lunch

12:30 p.m. Lunch

Time Blocks

60 min. Business building

45 min. Social media

60 min. Clean

20 min. Workout

5:30 p.m. Prepare dinner

6:30 p.m. Dinner

Time blocks help us so that we don't feel so stressed if we fall behind. Instead, we concentrate on completing our time blocks for each area. If we fall behind, I scheduled a catch-up time after lunch. I include clear time frames for certain tasks, such as waking, lunch, free time, and dinner, etc. This gives the family a guideline so that they can stay on track throughout the day. Since I don't schedule each minute of the day, they have more leeway when the unexpected inevitably occurs. By leaving cushions of time in my schedule, I allow room for the unexpected, which gives room for potential "free time." If nothing comes up, I have a list of chores or projects to complete during that cushion time. Honestly, if I were single and if I didn't have so many distractions in life, I personally would favor a very detailed schedule to keep me on task. My example just provides an alternative when it comes to scheduling.

You can find a ton of Apps to use for scheduling. I tried using one myself for months, but I just didn't like it. I thought maybe I was old school, and I needed to write my notes with an actual pen and use paper. However, a dear friend told me about www.any.do, a list-making app site that I found helpful. I knew it was going to work almost immediately. I didn't waste any time investing in the premium plan because it is so easy to use. I always leave the app open on my laptop. Every time I need to schedule something or make a list, the app is right there. I love it because I make lists and include my husband on a particular list so that he can contribute to it. It allows for time reminders, subcategories, attachments, and more. Basically, find what works for you or your family, be consistent with it, and watch it bear good fruit!

NOTES:

Chapter 8
Step 2 Creating Goals

Earlier, I wrote about creating a mission statement, and now, I would like to discuss creating goals. While your goals and your mission statement do impact one another, they are two different processes. Many people assume they already have goals because they know what they want to accomplish. However, the desire never seems to be enough to propel them toward accomplishing their goals. **A true goal is a desire to become or do something. Someone who wants to achieve a goal badly enough will work towards completion despite hurdles until they reach it.**

For example, many overweight people claim to have a goal of losing weight because they really would either like to be healthier or just more svelte. However, if they are not changing their lifestyle and their eating habits, not much will change. In my coaching classes, I tell my clients, "If you always do the same thing, you will always get the same result!" I often teach people the following principle: "If you can't change the way you eat, you can't change the way you think. If you can't change the way you think, then you can't change the way you live." Basically, our values and standards set not only a foundation, but also create a ceiling for our outcomes. If you have a low standard in any area of life you will find it impossible to reach above that standard. You might have lofty goals, but **your value system and standards determine whether your**

house will stand or fall when tough circumstances arise.
Think of the story of three little pigs. In the story, two pigs build a home with straw and sticks while the third pig builds his home with bricks. As you can imagine, the wolf blows down the first two homes while the third one stands firm.

What is your value system like? What are your standards made of? I am a very resolved person. Some days, I feel as if I am a walking standard. What do I mean by that? Plenty of times I will start to walk towards a room in our home and my kids will begin to scurry about to clean up. Why is this? It is because they know I have a standard and I want it to be upheld. Just recently I spoke to them about the importance of forming their own standards in every area of life, including HOUSE CLEANING. Anyone who has ever worked with me will attest that I am a women with high standards. It is always my desire to be the hardest worker on the crew and lead by example. So many people are easily bent, they are easily talked into or out of things. When people have solid standards they have made decisions ahead of time. They have decided where they stand on positions, they have decided what is important to them and most importantly they do not settle for less than the standard they have created for themselves.

We need to be sure that we are setting our standards and values before we launch out to set our goals. You need to set realistic quotas for yourself, a system that gives measurable results and accountability. You need to make some decisions about your health, your bank account and your friendships. You need to set a standard knowing that they are not made to be broken, but to keep and uphold! **When you are known for your high standards you will be known for your ability to reach your goals!**

Take a moment to think about your standards.
Do you have strong standards?

_____

_____

Do you stick to them?

_____

_____

Set Standards for:
Health:

_____

Finances:

_____

Friendships:

_____

Relationships:

_____

What you would like to be known for:

_____

_____

NOTES:

At the end of my country road as I was crying out I heard these words...

YOU CAN Do all things through Me, but I HAVE NOT called you to do ALL things...

- God

Anyone can dream, but each individual must make strategic plans to achieve their dreams and to accomplish what they set out to do. If you don't make a plan to reach your destination, you might get lost or worse, never arrive! Creating goals is really a form protecting your time which helps you to move closer to your mark rather than farther from it. Remember, when goal setting, use your mission statement as a guideline. Bounce everything off your statement and make sure that they both connect and align with each other. Another principle I live by is, "Don't work harder, work smarter!" Whenever I feel as though I am spinning my wheels and going nowhere, I go back to that expression. Goal setting with built-in accountability measures is not working harder but working smarter.

Also, remember to spend a lot of time looking in the mirror when you feel like you are hindered from accomplishing your personal goals. In life, you will face trials, but the select few will rise above the challenges that life brings, moving beyond their past hurts and current trials. I have heard many stories from people that have had far greater challenges than most people will ever experience in a lifetime, yet they have gone on to achieve their goals and make their dreams comes true. A special prize awaits those worthy of such determination. It goes to those who are willing to look themselves in the mirror and to say, "Other people have let me down, but I will not let myself down today. I am going to make a choice not to let the weaknesses of other people stop me from living out my dreams! No more excuses! Where there is a will, there is way, and I will find it!"

When you create your goals, list the strengths that you were born with. Each person was created with gifts and strengths that are unique to their calling. Recording your strengths will allow you to utilize what you already have available.

However, at times, we might be called into areas out of our comfort zone. We then need to acknowledge the areas that need growth and improvement to attain our goals. **Goal setting is life setting.**

1. **Steps to Goal Setting:**
    1. Start a goal journal – Use a journal specifically for goal setting and accountability. Of course, you can utilize computer documents or files to keep you on track. I find that writing goals on scraps of paper or in random spots will hinder the process. The point of goal setting is to create order, so utilize an organized method. For years, my husband and I have used spiral notebooks. I am always fascinated when I review old goal pages and see how things are lining up and how our focus has changed over time in some areas and remained the same in others. If you put your goals in a planner, choose one that has removable pages so that you can transfer your pages from year to year.

2. **List your strengths and weaknesses –**

Strengths:
Example:
Detail-oriented   I will write up a weekly schedule every Sunday night.

Strength	Accountability Statement
_____	_____
_____	_____
_____	_____
_____	_____
_____	_____

Weaknesses;
Develop a plan to **strengthen** your weaknesses.
Example:
Critical/Nitpicky   I will extend grace to others

Strength	Accountability Statement
_____	_____
_____	_____
_____	_____
_____	_____
_____	_____
_____	_____

3. **"Dream big"** – Create big picture goals. Focus on the far future, 10 years from now. What would life look like if money was not an issue?

   Would you own a home debt-free, would you like to have the freedom to travel annually and do mission trips? This is a perfect time to think about your calling and how to achieve life goals that will allow you to experience fulfillment in life.

   _____
   _____
   _____
   _____
   _____
   _____

4. **Set five-year goals** – These goals should focus on setting you up for your 10 year plan and be more realistic and measurable. If you are desiring to have a debt-free home in 10 years it might include saving a certain amount of money monthly or paying off consumer debt to focus on paying down a home loan. You might even look into Dave Ramsey's financial plan. My husband and I have been through the online course and we became debt-free by following his financial steps. Another finance plan that was very impacting and helped us to **stay debt-free** is **Jim Sammons Financial Freedom** video series. Dave's plan is about the nuts and bolts of getting debt-free and Sammon's series presents the heart behind staying debt-free for believers.

In five years it is my goal to:

_____
_____
_____
_____
_____
_____
_____

5 YEAR GOALS

When you can be known for your standards you will be known for your ability to reach your goals!

Use this page to write out your own personal meme, impact statement or draw a picture. Get creative. Come back to it to ENCOURAGE yourself.

5. **Set short-term goals**—annual and monthly—using the following guidelines: Goal, Plan of Action and Completion Date.
   Example:
   Goal: reduce debt. **Plan of action:** Attack one credit card a month and by paying the max I can or by setting a goal to payoff a card every 2 months. **Mark completion date.**

Goal:	Plan of action:	Date:

If you are visual you can make this really fun and interactive by putting together a vision board for your goals. You can even involve other people in the process by making this a group project and encourage each other as you work on your vision boards.

This section is what you will use on a regular basis to review your five- and ten-year goals semi-annually or as needed to make sure that you are staying on track.

After you decide on long-term goals, break these down into the smaller target sections so that you can reach your lifetime goals. Create topics for growth. After all, **growth and goals should be two sides of the same coin**. Areas for growth

might include:
- Spiritual
- Financial
- Marital/Family
- Career
- Health
- Education
- Physical
- Attitude
- Public Service.

Set realistic short-term goals because unreasonable goals lead to frustration, possibly even failure. I am not talking about doing away with big dreams. If you need to write a page containing your wildest dreams, by all means do that! However, just set realistic bite-sized goals to help you achieving your BIG dreams! Many years ago, I decided to base my goals on my personal performance. If I do my very best and if I give my all, then I know I am on track with my abilities. If I have learned one thing, it is this: tomato throwers in the bunch will always be ready to stop you from achieving your dreams because they are unhappy with their own lives and with everyone around them.

For years, my husband has been using the analogy of crabs in a bucket. We used to live on the coast near the beach, and we have seen a lot of crabs in our time. My husband always reminds us that you can put a bunch of crabs into a bucket and not worry about them climbing out because every time one tries to get out, another crab will pull him down so that he cannot ever escape.

You know the type of skewed thinking, "If I can't have it, neither can you." We have to be careful that we don't let the same kind of saboteurs do this to us. Instead, **create your own standard of measure based upon high self-accountability** or accountability within the framework of people you know who will give you honest feedback to help you succeed. If you follow that format, you will stay on the right track to success! If you solely base your performance on the opinions of others, you will become a people pleaser and find yourself very unhappy despite your best efforts. **Finding passion and purpose in life is about being the best and the most unique you that God created you to be.** So appreciate yourself, take care of you and combat self-rejection. When planning, create deadlines and end dates that allow you to celebrate accomplishments! I love to cross items off my goal sheet and to-do lists. This gives me a real sense of accomplishment and motivation. Remember that a written goal is as useless as the paper it is written on if you do not animate it and give it life and **power by** putting **your words** into **action**! **Consistency will be your best friend in time management.** Don't neglect this key aspect, or accomplishing your goals will suffer.

NOTES:

Chapter 9
Step 3: Creating Safeguards

Protecting your time and safeguarding your schedule should be of the utmost importance to you. If you do not take the proper steps and set-up a strategic mechanism to do so, you will inevitably squander precious time doing wasteful—or even good—activities because you are not doing what's needed to achieve your goals. In the end, you might be nearer to your goals, but your journey will be filled with frustration and agitation because you could have accomplished much more within that same time frame.

3 Steps to Fine Tune Your Schedule and Safeguard Your Time
  1. **Identify potential time stealers.**
     a. **Social Media**- Facebook, Twitter, Instagram, etc. The internet can rob our day. **Video Games** – On- and off-line. I understand that some people need an outlet for relaxation, but video games can be addicting. If you are addicted to video games, you will never achieve all that you desire to, period. They will hinder you from building strong relationships, and they will keep you from reaching your dreams.
     b. **Day Dreaming** – Not everyone has an issue with this, but many do. Typically, these people are nicknamed "visionary"—someone who is constantly dreaming of what could be. Yes, even day dreaming

in excess, without putting hands and feet to your dreams, can steal time! **Exchange daydreaming for cultivating and working toward BIG DREAMS!**

c. **Mr. Murphy** – Murphy's law states, "Anything that can go wrong, will go wrong." This fella has stolen a lot of time from most people. We have discovered that when we prepare for the unexpected, Mr. Murphy doesn't show up to the party.

d. **Laziness** – Loving sleep or slacking off can ruin a person's life. Typically, this correlates with entitlement and the feeling that others owe you; meanwhile, you put little effort into improving your life.

e. **The lack of planning and scheduling** – Remember the following sayings: "If you fail to plan, you plan to fail," and "If you aim for nothing, you will hit it every time!"

f. **Procrastination** – If you go through all the trouble to learn new tools for success and take the time to write out a schedule, only to put it off for another day, you, my friend, are a **self**-saboteur. I understand life happens, so plan for Mr. Murphy and build cushions to protect your schedule if you struggle in this area. The time for action is **now**!

g. **Not limiting phone time** – Schedule times to answer the phone instead of being available 24/7.

h. **Watching T.V.** – This can be just as big of a problem as social media. The habits of the wealthy do not include racking up hours of watching T.V. weekly to unwind.

Success Magazine had this to stay on the topic: "How much of your valuable time do you lose *parked in front of a screen? Two-thirds of wealthy people watch less than an hour of TV a day and almost that many—63 percent—spend less than an hour a day on the internet unless it is job-related. Instead, these successful people use their free time engaged in personal development, networking, volunteering, working side jobs or side businesses, or pursuing some goal that will lead to rewards down the road. But 77 percent of those struggling financially spend an hour or more a day watching TV, and 74 percent spend an hour or more a day using the internet recreationally."* "16 Rich Habits" by Tom Corley, September 8, 2016.[10]

i. **Distractions** – I have to admit that I struggle in this area. Even in school, my teachers noted on my report cards, "a pleasure to have in class, but easily distracted." Part of conquering the pull of distractions is by **not** multi-tasking! Yes, this is also hard because I was born to multi-task. However, multi-taskers are not more productive than those who focus on one project at a time. I admit that multi-tasking can be an addiction. Just as a "user" feels a euphoric moment of empowerment, so do pumped multi-taskers. However, the person then crashes and burns, leading to a vicious cycle!

j. **Failing to control your emotions** – Emotional stability will take you a long way in life. On the other hand, emotional instability will drain you and sabotage your day and result in a lack of

---

10
http://www.success.com/article/16-rich-habits. Accessed March 22, 2017.

productivity. Again, Tom Corley reports that 94 percent of wealthy people *filter their emotions.*[11]

NOTES:

---

11   http://www.success.com/article/16-rich-habits. Accessed March 22, 2017.

PASSION. PURPOSE. TIME MANAGEMENT.

10 TIME STEALERS
Our habits will reveal our weakness or our strength.

1. Social Media
2. Day Dreaming
3. Mr. Murphy
4. Laziness
5. Lack of Planning
6. Procrastination
7. Not Limiting Phone
8. Watching T.V.
9. Distractions
10. Failing to Control Emotions

Either you run the day, or the day runs you. -J. Rohn

_____

_____

Above list: Areas to erradicate or work on.

2. **Create an Accountability Statement.**

Identify your biggest time stealer/stealers and create an accountability statement. Write it out in your planner to remind yourself. You can check how much time you spend online by viewing your stats in your history log for the day or week.

Example: I realize that social media is consuming too much of my day, and I will not spend more than an hour daily utilizing it.

Accountability Statement:
_____
_____
_____

3. Utilize Your Schedule.
Not all potential time stealers need to be completely removed from your day unless you feel a conviction to do so. However, if you can't control your time when using them, cut them out!

    a. Schedule parameters for yourself as needed. If you need time to dream and conceptualize in your schedule, plan for that as well. Scheduling in time for Mr. Murphy has helped me because I feel less frustrated when he arrives. As I mentioned earlier, he visits less often when I am prepared for him. Give yourself cushions of time throughout the day to shrink and expand, especially if you are easily overwhelmed or discouraged.

b. Use a timer or watch and pay attention to the clock. This is where self-discipline comes into play. If you allow 20 minutes for an activity that might potentially steal your time, do not go over the set time! I am giving myself a reminder here too! We all need reminders sometimes.

NOTES

Chapter 10
The Power of Multiplication

What if I told you that you could multiply your time and duplicate your efforts? Would you do it?

Are you spinning your wheels and wishing for more time? Are you endlessly frustrated because the clock is perpetually ticking away while you are just struggling to make a dent in your endless to-do list? If so, one of the most powerful tools you can adopt is "The Power of Multiplication." In short, **duplication is multiplication**. They are **two sides of the same coin**. I didn't think much about this topic until 2008 when my husband and I attended a conference. A speaker there prayed over us, and she mentioned that our family has the "gift of multiplication." She confirmed many other things that were so completely right on that my life was forever impacted by her words. As time went on, I heard her words about multiplication echo in my ears, and I saw them come true in our family. Whatever we were involved in always grew tremendously and seemed to multiply. Looking back, I saw that part of our ability to multiply was in our desire to continually train people and share our life knowledge. It was our desire to duplicate what we know to help others be set free. Now that we understand the power of duplication, we have adopted a mindset that is focused on producing it.

MULTIPLICATION
&
DUPLICATION
are
two sides
of the
same coin...

When I first got married at 23 years of age, I was so hungry for self-growth. I wanted to be the best I could be for myself and for others. I started to read whatever I could get my hands on—books on time management, spiritual growth and inspirational material. Nearly 20 years later, I still fondly remember how those books impacted my life because they impacted my very being. I want this book to have the same kind of impact on your life! We are not born with a road map, but we can collect written works that will cumulatively change our lives for the better. I hope that this is one such book for you. Remember, life is what you make of it. **Choose to create the best story you can so that your journey can become a legacy.**
NOTES:

Mother's Day with my 7 children.

Let's take a look at some definitions I found in the Webster's Dictionary:

Multiplication- The act of multiplying or of increasing number; as the *multiplication* of the human species by natural generation[12]

Duplication- The act of doubling; the multiplication of a number by 2[13]

For this chapter, we are going to be considering these terms philosophically as opposed to literally.

In society, we are consumers. **Consumers deduct; they withdraw; they take away.** This goes directly against the principles of increase, duplication and multiplication. It is no wonder that our society is in the mess that it is in today! People are bankrupt, not only financially, but also in the big picture. People who are consumers raise kids who will become consumers. They will perpetuate the wasteful pattern until finally, there is no more!

A multiplier, on the other hand, is always looking for ways to give, to build, and to contribute.
They teach their kids the dangers of living as consumers. They teach them to give back to society rather than to take from it.

---

[12] https://www.merriam-webster.com/dictionary/duplication. Accessed March 22, 2017.

[13] https://www.merriam-webster.com/dictionary/multiplication. Accessed March 22, 2017.

Those kids teach their kids, and their kids teach their kids, and this impacts the future for the better! You can easily see the benefit in duplication if what you are duplicating has value and purpose. On the other hand, you can also duplicate a problem, a bad habit and poor choices. Some people might see it as a family "curse." However, I wonder how many of these issues are simply due to poor problem-solving skills and bad habits passed down from one generation to another. Duplicating in the negative will actually cause a greater deduction overall, a deduction in society, because it is impossible for poor choices to produce good fruit. This is not to say that beauty cannot come from ashes, but poor choices surely come with consequences.

NOTES:

A **MULTIPLIER**, is always **LOOKING** for ways to **GIVE**, to **BUILD**, and to **CONTRIBUTE**.

If you are unhappy or frustrated with your current life circumstances, ask yourself, **"Is it possible that I am duplicating in the negative?"** If you are feeling stuck, if you are feeling unsatisfied, you have probably been operating and building on the detractors in life rather than the multipliers! I mentioned **time stealers** earlier; these are often the root to **duplicating in the negative**. If we give into these time stealers every day and if we teach our family members or co-workers that this behavior is acceptable, we will duplicate these poor behaviors. The impact will spread across your household. **If you are in management, your whole organization will suffer** from allowing these detractors into your home or job site.

The real question is, "**What are you duplicating?**" Dig deep and throw your pride and ego out the window. Pride will lie to you and tell you exactly what you want to hear, which is what got you into this predicament in the first place. I know because that's what happened to me. It's hard for us to admit that we have wasted time and energy on habits, projects and relationships that have worked against us. If you struggle with an honest self-assessment, ask someone you trust to be truthful with you. However, make sure you find someone who will be totally honest with you and who understands your blind spots. Blind spots are called this for a reason. If a driver cannot see in a certain spot, he is blind in that particular area. For example, sometimes, we are investing so much into our own local community or even our church, that we overlook the needs of our own family.

Scripture states: "But if any provide not for his own, and specially for those of his own house, he hath denied the faith, and is worse than an infidel" 1 Timothy 5:8 (KJV).

Remember, you are a duplicator whether you like it or not, but not everyone is a multiplier in the positive sense! Please do not be so blind that you think putting your family after other humanitarian projects will cause positive multiplication in your household. Instead, it will cause a deduction in family relationships, which negatively impacts society. Why? Because what you duplicate will either build up or tear down. Building is multiplying while subtracting means tearing down. I have talked to and counseled so many people over the years who have been emotionally and spiritually broken because parents put people pleasing or material possessions and accolade over their families. Their kids are left feeling bankrupt, and many deal with numerous rejection issues. This is a drain on our society and on future relationships.

On the other hand, multipliers will look to better the future by focusing on what is truly important—they seek to bless others; they are not self-seeking or takers. They rise up when no one will stand, and **they are teachable**. They contribute to society and look to share the burden to make the world a better place in which to live. Most importantly, they place a high priority on relationships. When I think about that insight I received about our family being gifted in multiplication, I smile inside because we truly have focused on leaving an imprint on this earth, not just for our immediate household but also for our future generations. We are so focused on this goal that we bought 100 acres of land to build our dream—a community where our children are the main residents. We are not just thinking about ourselves; we are also looking to build a training center where people can visit our land, "Beth El Shaddai," and learn about sustainable living and holistic health. A dream is just a dream unless you give it legs, not to walk, but to run toward the goal.

Jim Rohn says, "You can't drift to the top of the mountain."[14] No, you are going to have to suit up and be prepared for the haul. Expect the unexpected and be ready for anything the elements can possibly send your way. When you reach the summit, you will feel a gratification that can only be felt when you worked hard to achieve something. No one will carry you to the top; you will only get their because you made a choice to stay the course, instead of turning around and giving up.

You have a clear decision to make, **"Are you going to be a multiplier and contribute to a better future for all, or are you going to duplicate your poor choices that will negatively impact the future?"**

NOTES:

---

[14] http://www.azquotes.com/quote/1334678. Accessed March 24, 2017.

PASSION. PURPOSE. TIME MANAGEMENT.

Chapter 11

When Passion, Calling and Time Management Link up

Finishing strong—how would you like to finish your life strong?

How would you like to go to your grave, knowing that you gave your all in every area of life and that if given the chance, you would do the same all over again?

How many people are really capable of even thinking such a thing?

How many people finish the race of their life, knowing that they gave the best of themselves in every area?

Regrettably, only a select few can have confidence and peace, knowing that although they made mistakes in life, they learned from them and went on to build upon the failings of life to rise up from the ashes! Most people end the story of their life filled with regret—regret that they did not love enough, have grace enough or forgive enough. They regret that they did not accomplish what they had hidden in their hearts for the whole of their lives. They did not accomplish what they were called to do. What lies behind is only shattered dreams and worse, dreams that were never pursued. What makes a winner in life? Is it the person that hid their faults and made excuses for their failings?
No. Is it the one that ended with the biggest bank account and

the most financial assets? Absolutely not.

Jesse Owens is known as one of the greatest and most famous athletes in track and field history. His 1936 athletic performance is remembered as one of the most outstanding performances in the Olympics. Jesse was born into a poor sharecropper family and started working in the fields at the age of 7. He was expected to pick up to 100 pounds of cotton in a single day. His family was so poor that when 5-year-old Jesse had a growth in his chest that was pressing on his lungs, his mother performed surgery on him herself. She did it because her husband felt it was the best decision. Jesse remembered his father's response to the in-home surgery, "I'm going to say it. If the Lord wants him...." However, the Lord had a plan for Jesse greater than just surviving the procedure that put his young life directly in the balance.

Growing up in a time of great racial tension, Owens was a black track star at Ohio State University (OSU), but he couldn't even live on campus nor eat there with his fellow teammates due to housing restrictions. Even so, he didn't let limitations set by others deter him from fulfilling his ambitions. He had a calling to break through the racial wall set up by others. He ran to break free. He ran because he was created to run. I picture Jesse running and can see it so clearly in my head. I am sitting in the bleachers surrounding the stadium that momentous day in history in 1936. I can feel his anticipation and the years of training culminating. He had worked so hard to put himself through college. All those years of dedication met him on the field on that pivotal day. I can feel his heart beating as he crouched down to take his mark.
I can feel the thick tension and energy in the air. Owens arrived on the track field that day, not just to win a literal race

by bursting through the finish line but also to break through twisted racial thinking. When he ran triumphantly past the finish line, he not only won on the field but also in the hearts of people who were looking for hope—hope for the future and hope for the world.

After the race, he wasted no time receiving the hand shake of his German opponent, Luz Long. On this eventful day, Owens stated, "You can melt down all the medals and cups I have, and they wouldn't be a plating on the 24-karat friendship I felt for Luz Long at that moment." Something was broken down that day and then built up, all in an instant. Jesse's call was to leave a mark on the world, and that he did. Jesse was a "class act"—a man who inspired a nation and became a cultural icon. To this day, he is remembered and honored for his ethics, inspiration and peaceful desire for equality. The need for accolade or medals did not propel Owens to go for the gold. He stated as much, "Friendships are born on the field of athletic strife and the real gold of competition. Awards become corroded; friends gather no dust."

It was not greed or pride that drove him but a strong desire to be all that he was created to be. When Jesse was 5, he laid on his parent's table, suffering with much loss of blood, covered by the prayers of his parents and the words of his father. "I'm going to say it. If the Lord wants him...." Even his parents could not fathom the plans that the Lord had for him that day. Jesse did not disappoint—he went on to become who he was created to be and left a lifetime legacy on humanity, and the echo of his name can still be heard long after his death in 1980.
Jesse went on to pursue his dreams amidst an oppressed era at a time when many felt hopeless and defeated. This young

man who did not live his life as victim of circumstance literally ran after his dreams to lay a stake in the annals of time. "We all have dreams. In order to make dreams come into reality, it takes an awful lot of determination, dedication, self-discipline and effort," said Jesse.

All these years later, Jesse's legacy continues. Jesse's great-nephew, Chris Owens, NCAA basketball standout, is carrying on the Owens' legacy and has also stated, "...Things happen on God's account." In 2009, Jesse's daughter, Marlene, made a public declaration that her father was "a husband, father, son, grandfather, friend, athlete, humanitarian, motivator, American and role model. He was loyal to each of these roles beyond expectation."[15]

Jesse personifies **what happens when passion, purpose and time management come together**. As Ephesians 5:16 reminds us, "Redeeming the time, because the days are evil" (KJV).
Are you redeeming the time? I can hardly imagine Jesse being stuck on social media all day or living as a victim of his circumstances, blaming others for his problems. Remember, no matter how hard you have it in life, someone will always have it worse than you. What kind of mark would you like to leave on this world? How much of what you are storing up can go with you when you die? What are you investing your time in? What a man sows, he will reap. What do you expect to get back for your time investment? Every day, we are faced with choices. Today, you do not have to feel lost; you do not have

---

15
       https://en.wikipedia.org/wiki/Jesse_Owens. Accessed March 22, 2017.

to face life without an action plan. You have been given tools to help equip you to become all that you were created to be. No one can choose how you manage your own personal time—that decision is up to you. You get to be the author of your life's story by the choices you make every day. Will your story be like Jesse's, who had a life filled with passion, purpose and time management? **Will you leave a legacy that's an example for future generations to follow, or will you leave a broken pattern? Will you be duplicating the negative or multiplying the positive**? You do not have the luxury of living a neutral life. Every life matters.

I believe very strongly in <u>the power of one</u>.

It only takes <u>one</u> person to <u>spark a flame</u> and to set <u>hearts ablaze</u>.

Not everyone has to be a track star to be remembered. No one has to be famous in this lifetime to make a mark.

All that you need to do is to understand that you possess everything necessary to be that one individual to create change! You need to believe that your life can make a difference for the world at large. Believe that your calling is sure, seek out your "what." Turn your search into finding and your finding into BEING who God has called you to be!

Know your purpose. **Know your "what"**. Know without a shadow of doubt why you were created, so that you can build on that sure foundation and **develop your "why"** upon it.

Not anyone else's. Your "why."

When you do these two things and submit yourself to Christ, your life's foundation will **not** soon be shaken.

Make a decision to pursue your highest calling.

Be intentional in all that you say and do. For it is written...

"So then each of us shall give account of himself to God." Romans 14:12

Live a life that will allow you stand before Yahweh and hear Him say, "well done good and faithful servant."

Make an intentional choice to be purposeful in all that you say and do. Aim to leave a powerful imprint on all the lives you come in contact with. Let your life be magnified so that when you walk into a room, they know change has arrived, not because you are so loud with your lifestyle, but because you are so committed to making a difference in the lives of others. Whether you are scrubbing homeless shelter floors or leading the masses in a triumphant march on Capital Hill, do it to magnify the love of Christ and His grace to others.

Remember,

Identify your "what."
Love selflessly.
Represent truth.
Seek to be your best for others.
Be gracious and humble.
Work hard.
Learn to love correction from others and God.

By doing these things you will grow like never before! These are the **keys to exponential personal growth**.

This brings a beauty that is far greater than what any plastic surgeon can ever provide—a tool that carves out a beautiful sculpture of the heart.

Make your life count, take back time, be focused and become intentional at creating the scenes you would like to see played out in your life story.

Choose to manage your time well and throw out the time stealers in your life.

You can live the life you want to be remembered for.

NOTES:

Keys to **EXPONENTIAL** Growth

Identify your **"WHAT."**

LOVE selflessly.

Represent **TRUTH**.

Seek to be your best for others.

Be **GRACIOUS** and humble.

Work hard.

Love **CORRECTION**.

PASSION. PURPOSE. TIME MANAGEMENT.

PASSION. PURPOSE. TIME MANAGEMENT.

I WILL
LIVE THE LIFE I WANT TO
BE REMEMBERED FOR...

These are the things I want to be remembered for:

_____
_____
_____
_____
_____
_____
_____
_____
_____
_____

Affirmation-Recite

I don't know about you, but I'm running hard for the finish line. I'm giving it everything I've got. No sloppy living for me! I'm staying alert and in top condition. I'm not going to get caught napping, telling everyone else all about it and then missing out myself.
1 Corinthians 9:24 (The Message)

Scriptures
Identity in Christ

2 Corinthians 5:17- Therefore if any man [be] in Christ, [he is] a new creature: old things are passed away; behold, all things are become new.

1 Peter 2:9- But ye [are] a chosen generation, a royal priesthood, an holy nation, a peculiar people; that ye should shew forth the praises of him who hath called you out of darkness into his marvellous light:

Ephesians 2:10- For we are his workmanship, created in Christ Jesus unto good works, which God hath before ordained that we should walk in them.

Romans 8:1- [There is] therefore now no condemnation to them which are in Christ Jesus, who walk not after the flesh, but after the Spirit.

John 1:12- But as many as received him, to them gave he power to become the sons of God, [even] to them that believe on his name:

2 Corinthians 5:21- For he hath made him [to be] sin for us, who knew no sin; that we might be made the righteousness of God in him.

John 15:5- I am the vine, ye [are] the branches: He that abideth in me, and I in him, the same bringeth forth much fruit: for without me ye can do nothing.

1 Corinthians 6:1- What? know ye not that your body is the temple of the Holy Ghost [which is] in you, which ye have of God, and ye are not your own?

1 John 4:4- Ye are of God, little children, and have overcome them:

because greater is he that is in you, than he that is in the world.

Romans 12:2- And be not conformed to this world: but be ye transformed by the renewing of your mind, that ye may prove what [is] that good, and acceptable, and perfect, will of God.

2 Timothy 1:7- For God hath not given us the spirit of fear; but of power, and of love, and of a sound mind.

Galatians 3:2 - For ye are all the children of God by faith in Christ Jesus.

PASSION. PURPOSE. TIME MANAGEMENT.

LIVE
the life
YOU
want to be
Remembered
for...

—EmmaSara

Thank you for taking time to read this book. I know your time is valuable and I am very grateful for your interest.

I would love it if you left a **book review on Amazon** and shared your feedback. Remember it only takes one person to spark a flame!

Thank you for your support!

About the Author

EmmaSara is a Compelled Lifestyle Expert; empowerment coach & speaker, integrative health educator, and executive pastry chef and owner of Compelled Bakery "A gluten-free bakery with a cause."

She is a lover of Yahweh and on her personal time she enjoys studying the Torah/Bible and exploring her family's 100 acre ranch with her husband. She has seven children that she is raising to be entrepreneurs and world changers! She is passionate about empowering the masses to "live the life they want to be remembered for."

Find out more at:
www.EmmaSara.com

www.facebook.com/CompelledLifestyle

Watch my **Compelled Lifestyle videos** on YouTube Subscribe to my channel or my playlists.
www.youtube.com/c/emmasaramcmillion

Follow me on Instagram @compelledlifestyle

To be **notified about my future releases,** email me and write **BOOK MAILING LIST** on the subject line. You will only be notified about book specials and new releases. Thanks for staying connected!

CompelledLife@gmail.com

Made in the USA
Columbia, SC
17 May 2017